WHO IS THE GOD OF HEAVEN?

JOHN BURKE

WHO IS THE GOD OF HEAVEN?

ANSWERS TO COMMON QUESTIONS ABOUT
NEAR-DEATH EXPERIENCES, GOD'S REVELATION,
AND THE LOVE YOU'VE ALWAYS WANTED

TYNDALE
elevate

Visit Tyndale online at tyndale.com.

Tyndale and Tyndale's quill logo are registered trademarks of Tyndale House Ministries. *Tyndale Elevate* and the Tyndale Elevate logo are trademarks of Tyndale House Ministries. Tyndale Elevate is a nonfiction imprint of Tyndale House Publishers, Carol Stream, Illinois.

Who Is the God of Heaven?: Answers to Common Questions about Near-Death Experiences, God's Revelation, and the Love You've Always Wanted

This booklet is adapted from *Imagine the God of Heaven*, published in 2023 under ISBN 978-1-4964-7990-7

Cover designed by Dean H. Renninger

Published in association with Don Gates of the literary agency The Gates Group; www.the-gates-group.com.

For information about special discounts for bulk purchases, please contact Tyndale House Publishers at csresponse@tyndale.com, or call 1-855-277-9400.

ISBN 978-1-4964-8019-4

Printed in the United States of America

29	28	27	26	25	24	23
7	6	5	4	3	2	1

Contents

Introduction

WE ALL IMAGINE GOD. Some imagine God as a myth or a fairy tale. Others imagine God as distant and scary, like a harsh judge or demanding parent. Still others imagine God as the most beautiful, loving, benevolent being in the universe. How you and I imagine God matters because it influences us, for better or worse, more than anything else we can think about.[1] It shapes how we view ourselves, others, and our very purpose for existing. That's why getting to know God is the most important thing we can do in life.

For more than three decades, I've been learning about God through studying the Bible, studying the world's religions and history, and studying over one thousand people who have clinically died, been resuscitated, and claimed to have experienced life after death.

Over the years, I became convinced that God is definitely real. Even more than that, God is relatable, and he is good! I believe that through near-death experiences, God is giving our global village evidence not only of his reality but also of the relentless and unconditional love he has for every single person on the planet. What I'm presenting can shed light on the most important questions of life: Who created me? For what purpose? What really matters? What is God like? What does God want with me?

Maybe you're going through a difficult time of illness or other suffering, and you question if God cares—or if he even exists. Perhaps you've lost a loved one, and in your grief you doubt that there really is life after death. Maybe you struggle with guilt and regret for choices in your past and wonder if you can be forgiven. Or perhaps you want to share hope with someone who is hurting.

Whatever your situation, I hope this little booklet, adapted from my full-length book *Imagine the God of Heaven*, will help you better understand the wonders of God: his epic story, his captivating character, and his love that is beyond our wildest dreams. Most of all, my hope is that you'll realize that all the love you've ever wanted, ultimately, is found in relationship with God.

What are near-death experiences (NDEs), and why should we study them?

Wayne is an aerospace engineer and lawyer in Australia who had a horribly painful heart attack. He floated out of his body, into a tunnel of light, and after traveling a great distance, he emerged:

> Into his presence, brighter than ten thousand suns—and I'm transfixed! It is awesomely beautiful. And I can see down into this light. At the center is the form of a man, arms outstretched towards me, like to welcome me and to hug me. At that moment, I entered, I merged with the light, and the light merged with me. Like when Jesus said, I am in you, and you in me [John 17:21]. I was like a glass container being filled up, filled up, filled up with him. And I was experiencing the most ecstatic love. It was bliss beyond belief, rapture beyond reason, ecstasy beyond explanation—love times a billion—but our word *love* fails so badly. Imagine every loving relationship combined all together, then blow them up billions of times all of that.[2]

Since the age of modern medical resuscitation and access to digital communication, more and more reports have surfaced across the globe about people being brought back from clinical death. A Gallup poll found that eight million Americans have had a near-death experience.[3] Oftentimes, people have a cardiac arrest, no heartbeat, and no brain waves, and yet modern medicine (or miracle) brings them back after minutes to hours of no registered brain activity. They come back to testify about an experience they say was more real than anything they have ever experienced on earth.

Every NDE is unique, just as every individual life experience is unique. Yet, despite the uniqueness and cultural filters of each, NDE accounts from around the globe share striking similarities, including often demonstrating a consistent order of common events. For instance, NDErs often observe their own resuscitation through an out-of-body perspective, travel through a tunnel or pathway, experience heightened sensations (such as brilliant new colors), feel overwhelming peace, see deceased friends or family members, and undergo a life review in the presence of a God of Light and Love.

What are these accounts? Are they actual scientific evidence for the soul and for God's existence? Or can

4

NDEs be explained by natural means, like the effects of a dying brain or anoxia or drugs?

Over the past thirty-five years, I've interviewed countless individuals and studied thousands of NDE reports trying to answer these questions. I've since become convinced that NDEs are God's gift to our world—evidence of God's great love for all people. That same evidence has also convinced many skeptical doctors over the years. I believe NDEs can help people who don't believe in God see that he's real, and they give color to the picture God has already revealed in the Bible.

How do we know that NDEs are true?

I've always been a very analytical, skeptical person. I studied science and engineering and worked as an engineer. I never liked the "blind faith" idea. I needed to have reasons to believe. NDEs opened my skeptical mind to the possibility of God being real, yet I still had my doubts. How do I know these NDEs are not just wishful thinking, or a trick the brain plays as a person is grasping to hold on to life? What about hallucinations, or the effects of anesthesia, drugs, or other chemicals flooding the brain?

There are several factors that lend credence to NDEs—and, further, lend credence to the existence of life after death. Here are just a few:

Verifiable observations. Thousands of NDErs claim they left their bodies at the point of clinical death, yet their person or soul remained in the room observing their resuscitation. These observations—frequently about specific things the medical personnel said or did during the moments of health crisis—are often surprisingly accurate, as multiple studies have verified.[4]

These kinds of observations have occurred even when a patient has no heart rate or brain activity. In some cases, patients whose eyes were covered during surgery or whose ears were blocked have reported seeing and hearing things they could not possibly have observed through their bodies, yet were later verified.

Heightened lucidity. Years and even decades later, NDErs consistently say their experience was more vivid, more real than anything they have experienced on earth. And this sets NDEs apart from other kinds of altered experience. Dr. Jeffrey Long points out, "In any other altered type of human consciousness—dreams, hallucinations, psychotic events—you typically have confused sensorium. Experiences may skip around in dreams, you really have that hypo—or decreased—lucidity, and that's completely different in near-death experiences, which are hyper or increased lucid experiences. And near-death experiences flow, and they tend to be very logical and ordered."[5]

Occurrence regardless of anesthesia or oxygen levels. A five-year study across multiple hospitals in Holland found that the occurrence of NDEs doesn't seem to be affected by whether or not a patient is under anesthesia, which suggests that NDEs cannot typically be attributed to medication in a patient's body.[6] The same study indicates that they're also not attributable to a lack of oxygen to the brain.

Meeting deceased people not previously known. Some people who experience NDEs report meeting someone who had previously died—including family members or others they had never met, yet were able to identify. For example, in recounting their NDEs, children sometimes describe meeting siblings who had died before they were born. Their parents had not told them about a miscarriage or a tragic death of a sibling, yet the parents verify what their children report about a deceased brother or sister they met during their NDE. Another example is from a woman who grew up thinking her stepfather was her biological father, until she met her true biological father in her NDE. Her mother later confirmed her discovery.[7]

Life change. In the Dutch study of 344 cardiac arrest patients, the experiences of a control group who did not report NDEs were compared to those who did report NDEs. Researchers interviewed all 344 patients two years after their cardiac arrest and then again eight years later. Here is what they found:

> The processes of transformation that had begun in people with NDE after two years had clearly intensified after eight years. . . . The people who had experienced an NDE during their cardiac arrest continued to be clearly different. In particular, they were less afraid of death and had a stronger belief in an afterlife. We saw in them a greater interest in spirituality and questions about the purpose of life, as well as a greater acceptance of and love for oneself and others. Likewise, they displayed a greater appreciation of ordinary things, whereas their interest in possessions and power had decreased.[8]

Numerous studies have followed the aftereffects of an NDE. If an NDE is not a real experience of a life to come, why would it change people's lives and perspectives so drastically?

The same God across cultures. NDErs come from vastly different cultures, religious backgrounds, and belief systems, yet they encounter the same God of Light and Love. I believe this is profound evidence not only of a life to come, but also of God's reality and identity. No alternative theories account for this or explain how people who did not believe God existed encountered the same God as those who did.

Surveys in thirty-five countries indicate millions have had an NDE.[9] Combine this sample size of millions with the prevalence of consistent elements, and you have strong evidence of a real life to come. There is a scientific principle: What is real is consistently observed. The consistency and prevalence of NDEs point to their veracity and the reason to try to understand their significance.

What does it mean that God is a God of love?

First John 4:8 says, "God is love." But it's hard for us to grasp what those words truly mean, and how that truth can shape who we become. I believe NDEs are God's gift to fill in with color the black-and-white words written in Scripture. Scripture reveals God's character and helps us understand God's love; NDEs can help us imagine what all of that means as we try to relate to God today.

Dr. Ron Smothermon had an NDE after being attacked and stabbed thirteen times by a mentally ill man who was visiting his home. As a Christian, he already believed in a God of love, but he was stunned by the overwhelming experience of that love during his NDE.

> God is truly glorious, magnificent,
> awesome, without equal. His glory is a
> light but made of infinite love. God's light
> appears like a sudden, silent, atomic bomb
> blast of white light, full of his power.
> Imagine being five feet away from the
> source of a nuclear explosion. But his light

is more than light—it is overwhelming,
a literal tsunami of infinite, unconditional
love. All it touches transforms into
perfect peace, and [it] blows away into
irrelevancy any consideration about what
is happening, replacing it with ineffable
ecstasy, irresistible joy, love beyond
comprehension—all in a singular
package.[10]

God's love story starts with God—the Person. And God is *personal*. God is not a force, nor is God "the universe." NDErs do not describe some impersonal feeling, but the love of a Person, even when their personal views, faith traditions, or cultures should have led them to expect an impersonal force or nothing at all beyond this life. NDErs experience a personal God who knows each individual more intimately than they had ever imagined—recalling things about their lives even they had forgotten. They all come back knowing that God is love, and that love is what matters most to God.

The apostle Paul also described the inexpressibly great love of God he wanted everyone to experience:

May you have the power to understand,
as all God's people should, how wide, how
long, how high, and how deep his love
is. May you experience the love of Christ,
though it is too great to understand fully.

EPHESIANS 3:18-19

God's love is so foundational that the big questions of life—*Why are we here? What is our purpose?*—can only be answered when we start to understand it.

You and I were created for a unique relationship with God. A relationship of love, unity, and cocreating with God. Unlike any other species, human beings have the capacity to create, care for, and develop God's creation in loving partnership with God.

The more you realize that God is the source of all love and that the love you've always longed for is ultimately found in God, the more you will want to seek God and trust him in faith. Nothing pleases God more. No other love compares to the love you are destined to experience when you trust in God.

How do we know that the God described in NDEs is the God we read about in the Bible?

The characteristics of the God that most NDErs encounter tend to be the same, no matter what nation, religion, or culture the individuals come from. NDErs consistently talk about God as being full of light and love, and both of those characteristics are consistent with descriptions of God that we read in the Bible. NDErs commonly report many of the characteristics of the God of the Bible, including experiencing the Father, Son, and Spirit, even when they had no prior knowledge of God's attributes. *Imagine the God of Heaven*, on which this booklet is based, reports many such cases.

In some cases, though, NDErs do express their experience of God in terms consistent with their respective religious traditions. If some NDErs say they saw Allah, or one of the millions of Hindu gods, or just an unnamed source of light and love, does this mean that there are multiple divine beings that nevertheless reveal themselves in similar ways in NDEs?

I don't deny that some NDErs claim to see their god or goddess, but it's critical to make a distinction between what they *report* compared to their *interpretations* of what they report.

Arvind, a Hindu from India, had a cardiac arrest and was taken to the hospital. He writes,

> I was given electric shocks. I started drifting upward. From a height, I could see my own body with many doctors and medical personnel working on my body. . . . Then I saw a huge light in the center of the hall, and I started drifting towards it. There was a huge light coming in from that huge hole. . . . I firmly believe in our Goddess, Mother Kaalika. I could feel that she was there on the other side of that beam of bright light.[11]

Arvind reported this brilliant light he knew to be divine, and he interpreted the light to be the goddess Kaalika. But consider how the goddess Kaalika, or Kali, is typically described. "Kali is most often characterized as black or blue, partially or completely naked, with a long lolling tongue [and] multiple arms."[12] What Arvind *reports* seeing resembles nothing like a black or blue, four-armed woman with her tongue hanging out, yet what he *describes* is consistent with the God of Light. This is commonly what I find. An NDEr may *interpret* what they saw as a certain goddess or god, but their *description* often matches the God of Light and Love described in the Hebrew Scriptures.

The Bible is full of references to God as light. For example, Jesus said: "I am the light of the world. Whoever follows me will never walk in darkness, but will have the light of life" (John 8:12, NIV). First John 1:5 says, "God is light; in him there is no darkness at all" (NIV). Throughout the Old Testament, God is a God of light as well. God appears to Moses as light like an undying fire (Exodus 3:2-3). Isaiah the prophet says that in heaven, "No longer will you need the sun to shine by day, nor the moon to give its light by night, for the LORD your God will be your everlasting light, and your God will be your glory" (Isaiah 60:19).

It is clear from Scripture that God wants his light and love to reach all people—including people from all religious and ethnic backgrounds. In fact, that's been his plan all along—to bless all the nations. About the time human history began to be widely recorded, God chose two people, Abraham and Sarah, through whom he would create a "chosen nation"— one set apart to bless all people in two ways. First, he revealed his heart, his character, and his will through many Jewish prophets so that we can know and love him as he loves us. Second, he made the incredible and radical prophetic promise that he would send the Messiah, the Savior for all humanity, to bless all nations for all time. NDErs around the globe meet this same God of Light and Love that Jesus claimed to reveal.

A Muslim Imam from Rwanda named Swidiq had an NDE as he was in the hospital facing a diagnosis of aggressive blood cancer.

> I saw sandaled feet and a white robe. In the presence of this man, I completely forgot about the [evil spirits], who fell back dismayed and then seemed to evaporate. I was captivated by him, totally uninterested in anything else but the sight of this person. . . . His face was serious and intent on me—the kind of expression that holds absolute authority—but the flicker of a smile or perhaps delight played across all his features. He stood a moment just looking at me. . . . At some point, he lifted his hands slightly, with palms up, revealing holes in each hand. Then he raised his right hand and gestured towards me. With lifted hand at last he spoke, clear and firm, "I died for

man. And you are among those I died for.
Do not deny it again. You must tell others.
Reveal it."[13]

Much like Jesus appeared to the apostle Paul when
he was persecuting Christians, God used this NDE
to reach Swidiq. He not only became a follower of
Jesus but is now an Anglican priest. And I believe God
uses other NDEs to introduce people from a variety of
faith backgrounds to the truth of who he is, in hopes
that they will seek him.

If God loves us, why does he allow bad things to happen to us?

We often assume that if God truly loves us, he will stop people from doing harmful things. God promises in Scripture that he will someday—all of the pain and suffering we experience is temporary. But for now, he allows humans the freedom to make their own choices.

The story of God's love recorded in the Bible is also the story of a fallen humanity, which is why parts of it can be confusing. The Bible records an unflinching record of the brutal realities of human behavior when we turn from God's loving ways and go our own ways.

God warned people about the consequences of a world created with the medium of free will. God says that our choices matter: "I have set before you life and death, blessings and curses. Now choose life, so that you and your children may live and that you may love the LORD your God, listen to his voice, and hold fast to him. For the LORD is your life" (Deuteronomy 30:19-20, NIV).

Much of the evil and suffering we experience right now is the result of people's wrong choices. And yet, while God allows us to turn from him and go our own way, he does not abandon us.

God is present and active behind the scenes of our world, sustaining all things (Hebrews 1:3, NIV). He is the source of all good gifts (Acts 14:16-17). God is also present on earth (unlike in hell), lovingly holding back evil's full expression through moral law intended to protect us.

In addition, God is present with us in a personal way through our own struggles. Several NDErs recount having a new understanding of how God had been with them during their times of suffering. A young girl named Melanie experienced a horrific sexual assault. Mercifully, God took her out of her body during the experience and comforted her. She remembered being up above, looking down at two men discussing whether she would live or die. As Melanie's spirit floated up above the scene, she suddenly realized Jesus was standing beside her.

> I really knew nothing about Jesus except
> what my babysitter told me. My parents had
> not taken me to church. But I intuitively
> knew exactly who this was: This was Jesus,
> and in his presence, I felt safe and loved. I
> had been scared in the dark, hearing the men

talk about whether I should live or die, but now with Jesus I felt safe. He said to me, "Don't worry. You're going to be okay." And it felt like he infused me with a peace or protection of his love.[14]

Melanie's NDE paints a beautiful picture of God remaining with us and comforting us even in the midst of terrible things. His love never wavers, and he never forsakes us. His love is stronger than any evil we can experience in this world.

The apostle Paul said it dramatically in his letter to the Romans:

> Can anything ever separate us from Christ's love? Does it mean he no longer loves us if we have trouble or calamity, or are persecuted, or hungry, or destitute, or in danger, or threatened with death? . . . No, despite all these things, overwhelming victory is ours through Christ, who loved us.
>
> And I am convinced that nothing can ever separate us from God's love. Neither death nor life, neither angels nor demons, neither our fears for today nor our worries about tomorrow—not even the powers

of hell can separate us from God's love.
No power in the sky above or in the earth
below—indeed, nothing in all creation will
ever be able to separate us from the love
of God that is revealed in Christ Jesus our
Lord.

ROMANS 8:35, 37-39

How can God's justice coexist with his unconditional love?

Love is the defining characteristic of God. However, he is also a God of justice and righteousness, and so he cannot excuse, ignore, or "wink" at sin or evil.

God described himself this way to Moses:

> Yahweh! The LORD! The God of compassion and mercy! . . . Filled with unfailing love and faithfulness. I lavish unfailing love to a thousand generations. I forgive iniquity, rebellion, and sin. But I do not excuse the guilty.
>
> EXODUS 34:6-7

Can you imagine the evil God sees daily across the globe? It angers God, and his love demands justice. God's anger is a temporary response when the people he passionately cares for abuse and harm themselves and one another.

When we witness or experience a wrong, we often accuse God of not bringing justice swiftly enough. But we also need to consider what God's swift justice might mean for *us*. What if God brought instant justice, not just to those who we think deserve it, but to every single root of evil, no matter how small, including our own? Who could survive God's justice? Many NDErs experience a life review, reliving their good and bad deeds and realizing how their actions affected God and others. They see their own wrongdoing much more distinctly in light of God's holiness. In God's presence, they feel the ripple effects of every right and wrong action with utter clarity.

From the beginning, God told us how he would resolve the tension between his justice and his love. God's justice cannot tolerate evil and sin, but his parental love would do anything to save the children he created. God had given the moral law, but the law was limited—it could restrain evil (with painful consequences), but it could not change the human heart. The core problem of humanity was disconnecting from God, the Source. Without being reconciled to the source of love, light, and life, we could not become who God created us to be, because he created us for relationship with himself!

So, God decided to do what the law could not do—God himself would enter into humanity as our Messiah, our Savior. He would pay the price his justice demands to freely offer forgiveness and restoration to all willing people. God revealed himself in a form we could relate to—God became one of us.

Before Jesus was born, God foretold how his love and justice would meet. Jesus would die for our sins, but he would conquer sin and death by his resurrection (see Isaiah 53). And through him, we, too, can overcome evil and death. We ask, "Does God care? Does God understand? Why doesn't God do something about all the evils, all the sorrow, all the brokenness?" He says, "I did! I entered into your poverty. I experienced your pain. I felt your rejection. I bore your sorrow. I took on the condemnation for all your wrongs. I paid the price of justice to purchase your peace with God, and by my wounds you can be healed."

This is God's solution to overcoming evil. Instead of destroying every little root and seed of evil in his outward justice, and thereby destroying all the people he loves, he pays for justice himself. God forgives and restores all people who turn back to him. As we lovingly walk through life with him, we become more and more the people he created us to be. He patiently overcomes evil in sometimes hidden ways, one willing heart at a time.

How do I pursue a relationship with God?

God created us to have a meaningful relationship with him, and he promises to be found by those who seek him with all their heart.

Santosh, an engineer who grew up Hindu, had an NDE where he saw the Kingdom of Heaven as a beautiful compound surrounded by high walls and twelve gates guarded by angels. He felt drawn to enter this place, but he intuitively knew the gates were closed to him. Then, he saw God, seated on a throne, powerful but full of love and compassion for him. On the left side, Santosh noticed a narrow gate into the kingdom that was open if God allowed him through it. God told Santosh he was sending him back, and when Santosh asked how to enter the narrow gate, he told him: "I want to see how true, how sincere, how honest you are with me, not just once a week, but every day, 365 days a year. How honest are you—that's the relationship I want."

After Santosh's NDE, he was confused about the identity of this personal, loving, relational God he had seen. This God did not match the Hindu gods of his background. But Santosh kept praying and searching for God with all his heart, trying to find answers to his questions: Who is this God of loving compassion? What does the mystery of the narrow gate mean? After two years of praying and seeking, he finally found what he was looking for.

When Santosh's daughter was invited to sing in an Easter choir at her friend's church, Santosh and his wife attended the service. "I immediately felt His presence, the presence of the very same Mighty Giant of Pure Light," Santosh recalls. "That day, the pastor was preaching a sermon as if he was talking to me. The sermon was on the narrow gate. He explained Jesus' words: 'Everyone who seeks, finds. And to everyone who knocks, the door will be opened.' Jesus said, 'You can enter God's Kingdom only through the narrow gate. The highway to hell is broad, and its gate is wide for the many who choose that way'" (Matthew 7:8, 13). Santosh was riveted as the pastor explained how Jesus is the gate and calls us his sheep:

> I tell you the truth, I am the gate for the
> sheep. All who came before me were thieves
> and robbers. But the true sheep did not

listen to them. Yes, I am the gate. Those
who come in through me will be saved.
They will come and go freely and will find
good pastures. The thief's purpose is to steal
and kill and destroy. My purpose is to give
them a rich and satisfying life. I am the good
shepherd. The good shepherd sacrifices his
life for the sheep.

JOHN 10:7-11

"I came back week after week, learning. And I
started reading the Bible," Santosh says. "I realized
that [He] was none other than Jesus Christ [whom]
I met in Heaven. Jesus is the one we can meet in the
human form of God. And I realized God *is* love—
that's what I experienced, and it's what I read in the
Bible."[15]

Santosh sought after God—and God was faithful
to his promise: "If you look for me wholeheartedly,
you will find me" (Jeremiah 29:13). Santosh found
God and gave his life to Jesus, trusting in his forgiveness and redemption. And those who do that begin
to know God not just as an idea or an entity, but as
a friend.

Friendship with God, walking with him by faith,
is how we grow up into spiritually mature adults. We

become people who do right things not out of religious obligation—to prove we are good—but out of the desire to love and please the God who loves us more than we can imagine.

What is heaven like?

The most emphatic and consistent comment from the thousands of NDEs I have studied is that there is absolutely nothing on earth—no experience we could imagine—that compares to being in the presence of God! All that we love here on earth is found in heaven, and in heaven, all creation is infused with the life, love, and glory of God.

Many NDErs recount the light and beauty of heaven. A nurse named Heidi described it this way:

> The grass was like the grass on earth,
> and the green was like the green of earth,
> but it was different as well. I realized
> that all the colors we experience here on
> earth are mere reflections of the colors of
> heaven. . . . The most beautiful perfect day
> on earth, while worthy and worthwhile
> and lovely, is still a pale reflection of
> every day in heaven. . . . I could see every
> single blade of grass. The most amazing
> part? . . . Each blade of grass was singing
> the praises of God. The music the grass

made was astonishing, amazing, gorgeous, heavenly, awesome.[16]

A man named Jim said,

I saw immaculately laid out concentric circles of golden streets, with greenbelts between them, and they intersected to form crosses. Streets of gold, but not like we think of gold. There was a translucent gold that you could see into almost like glass, but with a golden tint. Everything flowed to a brilliant light that appeared to be the throne of God. . . . The buildings were magnificent in scope and size, but there was a warmth to them—it felt like I had come home.[17]

Key passages in Scripture also reflect the beauty of heaven, describing mountains, rivers, a city sparkling like a precious stone, gates made of pearls, and a street made of gold, yet as clear as glass (see Revelation 21:10-14, 21; 22:1-2). In both NDEs and in John's vision of heaven in the book of Revelation, it's clear that what is experienced is far too wonderful to describe in words. Santosh said the city was built with "otherworldly building materials."

Beyond the beauty of the Kingdom of God, the key characteristic of heaven is the fact that God's presence permeates everything. Susanne, a nurse who had an NDE when she was young, said,

> Over the rolling hills, I could see this golden light growing. I thought it was a city behind the mountains. I knew there was a city and a throne, but I was focused on this beautiful, golden glow, growing and increasing, coming over the hills. I was captivated by this light because I just knew something magnificent was there. This was the presence of Almighty God.[18]

Many also encounter the person of Jesus. Fourteen-year-old Sarah said,

> There before me was the most BEAUTIFUL man I have ever seen in my whole life! . . . His eyes were wide with excitement and overflowing with LOVE and JOY. . . . There is no living person to ever exist that could match the BEAUTY of Jesus Christ. He was perfect in every sense of the word. He ran to me, and me to him. He embraced me and held me so close.[19]

God's presence brings an end to all sadness and sorrow, as well as great joy and delight. John says in Revelation,

> I heard a loud shout from the throne, saying, "Look, God's home is now among his people! He will live with them, and they will be his people. God himself will be with them. He will wipe every tear from their eyes, and there will be no more death or sorrow or crying or pain. All these things are gone forever." And the one sitting on the throne said, "Look, I am making everything new!"
>
> REVELATION 21:3–5

One of the greatest gifts of NDEs is the glimpses they give us into the reality of heaven—a place of inexpressible beauty where God's children live in the joy of his presence.

What happens to people who reject God? Is there really a hell?

Imagine that you are God for a moment. Because you are just, all wrongs must be made right. You're not like humans who live in the gray twilight of both good and evil; you are wholly *good*. "Only God is truly good," Jesus declared (Mark 10:18). You are the source of all good. The only thing that exists apart from you *is* evil. And hell is the place where you choose to stay out. Hell is where you give free-willed creatures what they demand when they don't want your love or leadership. Can you imagine how God feels?

It breaks God's heart to be separated from those he loves, but the just payment for rejecting God is giving people what they want—separation from God. And separation from God is death—not just physical death, but spiritual death—the "second death" described in Revelation 21:8. The apostle Paul put it simply, "For the wages of sin is death" (Romans 6:23), which is to be separated from God's love, light, and life. That's why God warns, pleads, and even begs us to admit our rebellion and just come home. Jeremiah 3:12-13 says, "My faithless people, come home to me again, for I am merciful. I will not be angry with you forever. Only acknowledge your guilt. Admit that you rebelled against the LORD your God."

When we reject his love and guidance, God feels the intense heartache of a betrayed spouse or a parent with self-destructive teenagers. During her NDE, Erica, a nurse, was shown God's intense sadness over any person who rejects him.

> Until now, I'd only felt the most over-whelming, unconditional love in the presence of God. Yet, now I was overcome by something else, a deep, aching sadness. The only thing on earth I could compare it to would be the death of a child. . . . I was feeling the death of a child multiplied millions of times over. It was then that I realized it was coming from God.[20]

Erica suddenly realized that God's great sadness came from losing his children—those who had rejected his love on earth.

According to one study, hellish NDEs are reported by 23 percent of NDErs.[21] While details vary, some NDErs see a place of utter darkness in contrast with the light of heaven. Santosh found himself on a high platform and saw a hopeless darkness and lake of fire infinitely far below, which he later discovered matched a description in the book of Revelation.[22] Jim, who was not a believer at the time of his NDE, experienced terrifying beings calling him toward hell.[23] Erica got a glimpse of both God's loving presence and what it was like to be separated from God and his goodness:

> The absence of His unconditional love was obvious. This was Hell. . . . They were criticizing and judging each other. There were angry and jealous conversations, full of gossip and spitefulness. These conversations were the exact opposite of the unconditional love and acceptance that emanated from God. Along with the conversations came . . . the most extreme emotions of sadness, anger, hatred, loneliness, jealousy, self-loathing, unworthiness, and everything you can imagine that was negative. . . . I can't even find a human word to explain the degree of sheer terror I felt.[24]

God wanted Erica to tell of the reality of both his infinite love for all people and his heartache over the reality of people choosing hell. Free will is necessary for love, and rejecting God's love and guidance has real ramifications, because justice must be served. As Oxford professor C. S. Lewis wrote, "A man can't be *taken* to hell, or *sent* to hell: you can only get there on your own steam."[25] Hell is justice for the free-willed creature who demands God "stay out." But God is good and God is love, so there exists in God a very real tension. His justice must allow the horrific consequences of rejecting God,[26] yet he loves us so passionately, he would do anything to have us with him eternally. He continually calls us to return to him, and through Jesus he demonstrated a love that laid down his life so that "everyone who calls on the name of the LORD will be saved" (Romans 10:13).

What about people who have never heard of Jesus?

Jesus said, "I am the way, the truth, and the life. No one can come to the Father except through me" (John 14:6). But what does that mean for those who have never heard about Jesus? Ultimately, Scripture does not tell us. What we do know is that God looks at the heart, he is just, and Scripture tells us that it is by faith, not by deeds, that a person is saved (Ephesians 2:8-10).

Salvation is found in no one but Jesus, as Acts 4:12 declares. Yet, according to Hebrews 11, many people who never knew the name of Jesus will be in heaven because of Jesus—among them Abraham, Moses, and Rahab—people of faith who lived before Jesus. God somehow applied Jesus' payment (which was then still to come) based on their faith in the light and knowledge they did have. Maybe God still does the same for those who have never heard his name today.

Jesus indicated that we may all be surprised by who is or is not in heaven: "Many Gentiles will come from all over the world—from east and west—and sit down with Abraham, Isaac, and Jacob at the feast in the Kingdom of Heaven. But many Israelites—those for whom the Kingdom was prepared—will be thrown into outer darkness" (Matthew 8:11-12). It's not for us to judge who will or will not be saved by God's amazing grace.

Dean Braxton was a Christian when he had an NDE. He was shocked to see his aunt in heaven. "With my belief system, I had her in hell, I'll be honest with you. There she was in heaven. I came to understand it wasn't up to me. It's up to Jesus. Sometimes we may make a judgment over a person, but that's between them and God. He knows. Then I came to understand it didn't matter if I knew. It mattered if he knew."[27]

Scripture states, "The eyes of the LORD search the whole earth in order to strengthen those whose hearts are fully committed to him" (2 Chronicles 16:9). God wants all people to hear and know about his love and forgiveness offered through Jesus. He does not want us to live condemned by our sin, in fear of death or judgment. Instead, he wants us to live in the confidence of knowing we are in right relationship with God, now and forever.

39

How do I know that God hears my prayers?

Jim was a former commercial airline pilot who had developed Guillain-Barré syndrome, a severe auto-immune disease that attacked his nervous system, causing excruciating pain that left him increasingly dependent on opioid medication. One night in his truck he took too many pills, collapsed, and died. His medical records report eleven hours with no brain activity.

Two of Jim's sisters-in-law were woken up that night with an urge to pray for Jim, and Jim's wife and other family members prayed fervently as well. Jim recounts what he saw in heaven during his NDE:

> I looked up in the sky, and it was a cerulean blue—it was a sunless sky, deep, deep blue, and I spotted something like streaks of brilliant light going straight up. [To me] as a pilot, they looked like the white contrails of ice left behind by jets. I thought, *Are those contrails?* I was stunned, seeing six contrails across the sky. I asked the Guardian, "What

are those?" And he said, "James, those are the prayers of your family for your soul, as we speak." When I got back, I found out my family all came to the house and six of them prayed, "If it be the will of Jesus, please send Jim back." And I was in Heaven seeing those prayers.[28]

Your prayers matter to God. God not only attends to every single prayer of every person; God answers our prayers in such a way that the outcome works together for our good *and* for the good of all those who love him (Romans 8:28).

I find it encouraging to know that we don't even have to "do it right" for God to hear or answer our prayers. Prayer is not a puzzle or a formula, something we have to figure out with precision before God will hear us or give us what we ask for. Prayer is simply communicating with God—silently in our hearts or out loud. In prayer, we have a conversation with God, our Creator, who loves us and wants to guide us through life by his Holy Spirit. We don't have to be good at prayer, we simply have to be willing to do it! God promises his Holy Spirit will help us—aligning our will to God's will as he works all things together for good.

The Spirit helps us in our weakness. We do
not know what we ought to pray for, but
the Spirit himself intercedes for us through
wordless groans. And he who searches our
hearts knows the mind of the Spirit, because
the Spirit intercedes for God's people in
accordance with the will of God.

ROMANS 8:26-27, NIV

Not one tear, struggle, question, or heartache
taken to God in prayer is lost on him. In fact, the
promise of Scripture is this: "You keep track of all
my sorrows. You have collected all my tears in your
bottle. You have recorded each one in your book"
(Psalm 56:8). He holds our tears as treasures when we
call out to him in prayer through the valleys of life.

Is there a purpose for suffering?

Mark was only a teenager when he sustained terrible burns over 65 percent of his body during a house fire. During surgery, with the anesthesia not working, still in unbearable pain, Mark's heart stopped. He says,

> I felt the presence of God—a love that is just so difficult to put into words, but a sense of love and security that's almost indescribable. Everything is okay. It always has been, it is now, and it always will be, and there's nothing to be afraid of.[29]
>
> All things—past, present, and yet to be—had a specific purpose and reason. . . . Everything was perfect, exactly as it was intended from the beginning of time and would remain so forever. And all of this was so plainly apparent that I felt like giggling at the simplicity and impeccability. *Oh . . . God! Of course! Who else?* It was wonderful to be free from pain, but even that which I'd experienced did not matter anymore. And

it was hard to even categorize it as bad. . . .
*No suffering is ever in vain. All pain has its
purpose and is part of the plan.*[30]

Mark survived the surgery and endured a long
recovery, as well as a number of other heartbreaking
losses and challenges in his life. He is honest about his
struggles, but even years later he affirmed his belief in
God's goodness and his plan:

God wants us to know we can do anything
with His help. He will help us through
anything, but He doesn't just dump stuff on
us so we can prove how strong we are. He
does that so we can be sculpted and molded
and forged into the being and character He'd
like us to be. . . . I want people to realize the
joys far outweigh the pain, and it's worth
it. . . . I've had such a good life.[31]

What makes suffering "worth it"? For most of
us, it's the sense that our suffering is contributing
to something better. Whether that's developing character in us, drawing us closer to God, or giving us
more compassion for others in their own struggles,
we all want to believe that our pain is a piece of some

greater plan. And Scripture tells us that is true. One of the mysteries of faith is that God allows humans to have free will but also somehow accomplishes all of his purposes. In the Old Testament book of Isaiah, we read:

> I am God, and there is no other; I am God, and there is none like me. I make known the end from the beginning, from ancient times, what is still to come. I say, "My purpose will stand, and I will do all that I please."
>
> ISAIAH 46:9-10, NIV

God makes it very clear that he has a plan and purpose—and what he has planned will happen. Knowing the loving character of God, you and I should have lots of assurance about the future as we follow him. Nothing can thwart his will or his ultimate plans and purpose.

The apostle Paul reiterates this truth, saying, "In all things God works for the good of those who love him, who have been called according to his purpose. For those God foreknew he also predestined to be conformed to the image of his Son" (Romans 8:28-29, NIV). Even when our circumstances are confusing and life is not going the way we hoped, we can rest assured that God's plan for us is good, and ultimately it is to help us become more like Jesus. So we should pay attention to what God is doing *in* us, not just around us. He can turn the hard things in our lives into something beautiful.

Why doesn't God make himself more visible to us?

If God loves us so passionately, we have to wonder, why does he often seem to hide? Why does he ask us to seek him so diligently and then show up in ways that seem obscure or mysterious? As I've wrestled with these questions, I've concluded that our relationship with God while we're on earth is something like an engaged couple living in separate cities—we long for the day we will be united as one, but that day is yet to come. God wants to know, "Will your heart grow cold or stay faithful? Will you read the messages I send, or get busy and forget about me?" But he also promises that he will not abandon those who search for him (see Psalm 9:10).

Some of us may read stories of NDEs and feel envy, wishing we could have such a wonderful experience. We might even feel that if we could see God so clearly, we might never doubt again. But after hearing so many NDE stories over the years, that's not what I've found.

While many NDErs are drawn closer to God after their experience, I've interviewed some who write about being overwhelmed by the unconditional love and compassion of this God of Light and may even experience Jesus himself, yet they then turn away from seeking God. Some even deny Jesus, pursue other supernatural encounters, or seek to recreate the experience rather than seek the God of the experience. We also see in the Bible that some of those who witnessed great miracles of God—the Red Sea dividing to allow the Israelites to escape from the Egyptian army, the walls of Jericho falling down, Jesus raising Lazarus from the dead—eventually turned away from God or hardened their hearts to him. Those who say they won't believe because they lack proof often don't *want* to believe, and they won't believe even if proof comes. As Jesus said in a parable, "If they do not listen to Moses and the Prophets [the Bible's words], they will not be convinced even if someone rises from the dead" (Luke 16:31, NIV).

God wants us to trust him, and he says we're blessed if we believe even when things aren't completely clear. Orthopaedic surgeon Dr. Mary Neal had an NDE when she was pinned in a kayak under a waterfall for thirty minutes. After seeing Jesus, she told him, "This is wonderful. Why don't you do this for everyone, and everyone would believe?" Jesus quoted himself, "You see and believe, but even more blessed are those who don't see, yet believe."[32] He paraphrased his own response to "doubting Thomas" as recorded in John 20:29.

I find that God does not often reveal his identity during an NDE, except with hints or clues, reminiscent of how Jesus taught in parables. He wants to know if we will seek to know him. The promise of Scripture is, "If you search for [God] with all your heart and soul, you will find him. . . . You will finally return to the LORD your God and listen to what he tells you. For the LORD your God is a merciful God" (Deuteronomy 4:29-31).

Is God really willing to forgive me?

What is the message of Jesus? NDErs may have differing interpretations about that, but Jesus clearly told us his main message, called the *gospel* (which means "good news"). The gospel is how he demonstrated his universal love for all. When he appeared to his followers after his resurrection, he said,

> It was written long ago that the Messiah would suffer and die and rise from the dead on the third day. It was also written that *this message* would be proclaimed in the authority of his name to all the nations, beginning in Jerusalem: "There is forgiveness of sins for all who repent."
>
> LUKE 24:46-47, EMPHASIS ADDED

The word *repent* simply means to turn back to God. That's the message, his good news for all people. Forgiveness is available for all who turn back to God.

Without understanding the message of what God did for us through Jesus, we tend to either live under the weight of judgment and shame (knowing we sin and fall short but feeling responsible to try harder in our own power), or we harden our hearts and run from God. So, God made another way forward through the death and resurrection of Jesus.

Paul explained what God accomplished for us that day: "God made you alive with Christ, for he forgave all our sins. He canceled the record of the charges against us and took it away by nailing it to the cross" (Colossians 2:13-14). That's the message of Jesus. For all who want forgiveness and freedom from the burden of guilt, he says, "You're forgiven. I'm not against you, I'm for you!"

A woman named Alexa had an NDE when she lost great quantities of blood after delivering her second child. Her story provides a wonderful picture of how condemning accusations can't stand against the truth of God's grace. She describes her life review, which took place in a sort of courtroom:

> EVERYTHING I ever thought, did, said, hated, helped, did not help, and should have helped was shown in front of me. . . . How mean I'd been to people, how I could have helped them. . . . It was horrible. I fell on my face in shame. I saw how my acting, or not acting, rippled in effect toward other

people and their lives. It wasn't until then that I understood how each little decision or choice affects the World. The sense of letting my Savior down was too real. Strangely, even during this horror, I felt a compassion, an acceptance of my limitations by Jesus and the crowd of Others.

During this Review, the Evil being was there. . . . I shrank back in horror. Every time during the Review that I erred or failed, he enjoyed it immensely. He would shout out, "THERE! See how she messed up?" He would accuse me, "Why didn't she do better? Or help more? She ought to be punished!" I was desolate. My few, little good works didn't and couldn't measure up to God's perfect standard.

Then, when it was over, a huge deep voice boomed out: "IS SHE COVERED BY THE BLOOD OF THE LAMB?"

"YES!"

With that, Jesus looked at Satan and declared: "SHE'S MINE!" . . .

Everything in that setting was gone, except the Heavenly crowd and Jesus Christ. He gazed at me with INCREDIBLE love!

He held out his nail-pierced hands and wrists, that although healed completely, had the outline of the crucifixion marks. . . . He spoke of who He was, and that He was my advocate with God the Father. I fell down in awe and worshiped Him with my very Soul. I cried with Joy like a baby as I gazed up at His glorious, loving smile. He loved and accepted me—totally. I was filled with peace and contentment.[33]

Jesus' death on the cross paid for your forgiveness for your past, present, and even future wrongs. If you tell God you want his forgiveness offered through Christ, you stand forgiven! The apostle Paul writes, "So now there is *no condemnation* for those who belong to Christ Jesus. And because you belong to him, the power of the life-giving Spirit has freed you from the power of sin that leads to death" (Romans 8:1-2, emphasis added). God wants you to live free, now and forever.

What is worship? Why is worship a natural response to God?

NDErs have an opportunity to see the glory and power of God in a way that the rest of us can only imagine, and it can have a profound effect on them. They often respond with spontaneous worship, even if worship felt foreign to them on earth.

When Dean Braxton had his NDE, he experienced the presence of Jesus and felt the magnificence of God and his throne in exhilarating ways:

> I came up on the side of [Jesus]. I looked at his feet, and when I looked at his feet I saw the holes—not in the feet but the ankles. . . .
> All I could think of was, *You did this for me.*
> I dropped to my knees saying, "Thank you, thank you, thank you." . . .
> No matter where I went in heaven, God was there. . . . The glory of God is shining out of everything. . . . In heaven, I experienced "the fear of the Lord" [described] in Scripture. It is a sense of awe and respect. He's so pure—all these words don't seem right—so clean, nothing wrong, no evil, all so pure. It is holiness.[34]

Throughout Scripture, we see people changed when they encountered God. They were filled with awe when they got a glimpse of who he really is. When the apostle John saw the resurrected Jesus during his vision of heaven—with eyes like flames of fire, a voice thundering like ocean waves, and his face shining like the sun—he fell at Jesus' feet (Revelation 1:12-18).

The power of God reminds us just *who* this infinitely kind, loving being is—the one who deserves utmost honor, respect, awe, and even fear if it were not for his great love. It's not that we *should* or *ought* to feel awe and respect, but that we *will* on the day we experience God as these NDErs have. And properly imagining God in all his power helps us to grow in loving awe and respect for God today.

A thirty-three-year-old woman named Crystal had an NDE when she coded in the hospital due to complications from pancreatitis. She had no heartbeat or brain waves for nine minutes.

> I was . . . aware of a being on my right, and
> instantly I knew who this was, too. And
> what overcame me was a profound, endless
> desire to praise and worship this being, for I
> knew immediately I was in the presence of
> God. . . .

The sheer ecstasy of it! The beauty
of it, the joy and the grace, the way my
spirit soared and my heart burst—how I
wish I had the words to convey just how
miraculous this was. . . .

With every fiber of my existence I
wanted to praise and worship God, and
that's *all* I wanted to do. And I wanted to
do it *forever*. . . . What drove my praise was
the intensity and immensity of my love for
God. There is simply no other love remotely
like it.[35]

Around the throne, the worship of God the Father
is not a "should" or an "ought," but something that
erupts out of a joy and ecstasy that NDErs say they
just can't contain. They never want to stop—that's
how wonderful it is to be with God.

Revelation 7 presents a glorious picture of those
in heaven worshiping God together:

After this I saw a vast crowd, too great to
count, from every nation and tribe and
people and language, standing in front
of the throne and before the Lamb. They
were clothed in white robes and held palm

branches in their hands. And they were
shouting with a great roar, "Salvation comes
from our God who sits on the throne and
from the Lamb [Jesus]!"

REVELATION 7:9-10

Imagine all the awesome wonders and mysteries
we have ahead of us as we experience eternal life in
God's presence. Maybe imagining such heavenly wonders can help us join all creation in praising him now!

What really matters to God?

When we think of God's plan or purpose for our lives—what he says matters most—we usually think first about careers or accomplishments that would seem noble or important. I'm convinced that although that matters, it's not central to God's plan for your life. Based on multiple NDEs, much of God's plan appears to be about the *people* we will meet *along our path*.

NDEs confirm what the Scripture teaches: God's plan seems to first center around who you become in relationship to God and how you impact those around you. Secondarily, God's plan is about what you do to serve humanity through your gifts, time, and resources. This reflects what Jesus said when he was asked to identify the most important commandments: "'Love the Lord your God with all your heart and with all your soul and with all your mind.' This is the first and greatest commandment. And the second is like it: 'Love your neighbor as yourself.' All the Law and the Prophets hang on these two commandments" (Matthew 22:37-40, NIV). We fulfill our purpose when we love God and love those around us.

Erica, the nurse we read about on pages 35–36, mentioned how through her NDE, God allowed her to review her life from his perspective and see what matters most to him.

I saw myself helping an elderly person
with their groceries, comforting a friend in
need, saying something kind when others
were mean, standing up for the unwanted,
advocating for those who couldn't find their
voice, and being a patient listener to those
who desperately needed to be heard. . . .
I felt the immediate effect of my words,
thoughts, and actions on others. A great
majority of these things I did not remember
I had done because they were mostly things
I did when no one was looking. But God
was looking. I understood in that moment
that these things were displays of love,
kindness, and compassion. They were the
only things that mattered in God's eyes.
They all required love. Love was the answer
to everything![36]

Our words and actions matter. When we love God, walk with him, and reflect his love and joy to others, we are fulfilling our purpose and doing what matters most to God.

How do we stay connected to God through the Holy Spirit?

The night before his crucifixion, Jesus explained to his disciples how he would guide them when he was no longer with them, giving an analogy of the one thing that matters most for spiritual growth:

> A branch cannot produce fruit if it is severed
> from the vine, and you cannot be fruitful
> unless you remain in me. Yes, I am the vine;
> you are the branches. Those who remain in
> me, and I in them, will produce much fruit.
> For apart from me you can do nothing.
>
> JOHN 15:4-5

We grow spiritually by staying connected to God moment by moment in our thoughts. It's how we become who God created us to be and how we accomplish our God-given purpose.

The apostle Paul calls this "walking by the Spirit" and explains the spiritual fruit that grows as a result: "So I say, walk by the Spirit, and you will not gratify the desires of the flesh [old sin-habits]. . . . But if you are led by the Spirit, you are not under the law. . . .

The fruit of the Spirit is love, joy, peace, forbearance [patience], kindness, goodness, faithfulness, gentleness and self-control" (Galatians 5:16, 18, 22-23, NIV). Do you see what this says? Do this one thing—walk by the Spirit daily—and you don't have to white-knuckle in your own effort to "stop this" or "try harder" to quit that, or muster up more religious effort to "be good." God grows good fruit from within, naturally.

Here's the key question: What do you set your mind on? All through the day, do you let God's Spirit into your thoughts? Do you talk over your thoughts with God's Spirit? Or do you give your attention to old ways of thinking, such as lies and negative or condemning words that may have shaped you in the past or are shaping you now?

Paul described the process of spiritual growth and living in the Spirit when he wrote, "Don't copy the behavior and customs of this world, but let God transform you into a new person by *changing the way you think*. Then you will learn to know God's will for you, which is good and pleasing and perfect" (Romans 12:2, emphasis added). You live in the Spirit when you make it a habit to go through your day, moment by moment, inviting the Holy Spirit into every thought, every decision, every action. You listen for the quiet prompting of the Spirit, allowing him to align your thoughts with the truths of Scripture, so you can know what is true. Then you can follow his lead when he prompts you to keep quiet, speak up, or take action.

At the end of Heidi's NDE (see pages 30–31), as she was returning to her body, she felt Jesus' presence still with her. She says,

> Jesus left, but he left me with his Presence.
> I couldn't see him, but he was there. I felt
> his Presence and his Presence reassured me.
> Over the years, his Presence made me want
> to know more—to seek Jesus. To seek him
> physically in Israel, and then to seek him
> in Scripture, and ultimately in community
> [a synagogue and a church]. What I would
> now call the Holy Spirit changed my
> present life.[37]

The more you act in faith on the Holy Spirit's promptings, the more you'll look back and see God working in your life.

How does life with God bring us joy?

There is one attribute of God often overlooked by theologians, miscalculated by most people, yet clearly revealed in Scripture—God's eternal joy! Failing to imagine God as the source of all our joy and laughter, fun and games, pleasures and enjoyments of life has led many people to turn away from God. But we should be running toward God if we desire to enjoy life fully!

Rebecca Springer lived in the late 1800s and had what we would now consider an NDE after being very ill, possibly with pneumonia. She wrote extensively about joyful reunions with her deceased parents and other family members; seeing children and pets playing; hearing angelic music; and meeting Jesus. Rebecca later reflected that compared to earth's joys, "there is a depth, a mystery to all that pertains to the divine life, which I dare not try to describe. . . . Suffice it to say, that no joy we know on earth, however rare, however sacred, can be more than the faintest shadow of the joy we there find."[38]

Several NDErs mention laughter as part of their experience—even laughing with Jesus himself. God is the most joyful being in all of creation. Yet joy is a characteristic of God that we don't often imagine. How could we miss it? All our enjoyments and pleasures are in fact *his creations*. And God wants us to include him in the enjoyments of life he has provided. One of the greatest lies of evil is the upside-down idea that laughter and fun, pleasure and thrills, and all the really fun parties are found apart from God. We need to infuse our imaginations with truth—no one enjoys life with his children more than God.

Does God also grieve, suffer with those who suffer, and get angry at our injustices? Yes! But all of those are temporary reactions to an evil world. Joy is God's eternal default state! God tells us, "Be glad and rejoice forever in what I will create, for I will create Jerusalem [heaven's New Jerusalem] to be a delight and its people a joy. I will rejoice over Jerusalem and take delight in my people; the sound of weeping and of crying will be heard in it no more" (Isaiah 65:18-19, NIV).

If you follow Jesus, joy is your birthright. You are a child of the king of all joy! Joy is where you are headed, joy is what you'll inherit, joy is the norm, and God's joy is available to you, even now. In fact, you can experience the eternal now of God's joy regardless of trials, through tribulations, no matter what circumstances surround you. As a child of God, joy is available because God is with you, and God *is* joy.

What motivates us to share God's love with others?

The other night, my neighbor had a party and about fifty people on our street came. It looked like the United Nations gathering as I talked to my neighbors from India, Pakistan, Israel, Korea, China, and from across the United States. It was a wonderful time, great food, fun, and laughter. My wife, Kathy, and I had some awesome conversations, even sharing about writing this book and how God is better than any of us could ever begin to imagine.

God is pleased when our neighbors get to know each other, when they learn to care more about one another, and when someone tells them of God's immense love for them. My prayer since that party has been, *God, move the party to heaven! I want all my neighbors to come to your eternal party.*

His last night on earth, Jesus told his closest friends that they would celebrate and feast together again, but "I will not drink wine again until the day I drink it new with you in my Father's Kingdom" (Matthew 26:29). Jesus described heaven as a celebratory feast:

The Kingdom of Heaven can be illustrated by the story of a king who prepared a great wedding feast for his son. . . . "Come to the banquet!" [the servants of the king declared]. But the guests he had invited ignored them and went their own way. . . . And he said to his servants, . . . "Now go out to the street corners and invite everyone you see." So the servants brought in everyone they could find, good and bad alike, and the banquet hall was filled with guests.

MATTHEW 22:2, 4-5, 8-10

God's Kingdom is an open party—everyone is invited. Regardless of what we've done, good or bad, he is the one who makes us worthy of his eternal party. But we need to accept his invitation—and share it with others. Will you invite God into your gatherings, thanking him, loving those he puts in your path, telling them how much God cares for them?

God is infinitely greater than you or I can imagine, in every way. His grand love story will never end but truly begins with people from all nations united with God in a joyful celebration like earth has never seen.

Notes

1. In his book *The Knowledge of the Holy*, author A. W. Tozer put it this way: "What comes into our minds when we think about God is the most important thing about us."
2. Wayne Fowler, Zoom interview with John Burke, November 1, 2021. Used with permission.
3. "Near-Death Experiences Illuminate Dying Itself," *New York Times*, October 28, 1986, https://www.nytimes.com /1986/10/28/science/near-death-experiences-illuminate -dying-itself.html.
4. Janice Miner Holden, "Veridical Perception in Near-Death Experiences," in *The Handbook of Near-Death Experiences: Thirty Years of Investigation*, ed. Janice Miner Holden, Bruce Greyson, and Debbie James (Santa Barbara, CA: Praeger, 2009), loc. 2788, Kindle.
5. Jeffrey Long, MD, personal interview with John Burke, Austin, Texas, October 2, 2019.
6. Pim van Lommel, "Non-Local Consciousness: A Concept Based on Scientific Research on Near-Death Experiences during Cardiac Arrest," *Journal of Consciousness Studies* 20, no. 1–2 (January 1, 2013): 12–14. See also Dr. Pim van Lommel, Ruud van Wees, Vincent Meyers, and Ingrid Elfferich, "Near-Death Experience in Survivors of Cardiac Arrest: A Prospective Study in the Netherlands," *Lancet* 358 (December 15, 2001): 2039–2045, https:// www.thelancet.com/pdfs/journals/lancet/PIIS0140 -6736(01)07100-8.pdf.

7. Van Lommel, "Non-Local Consciousness," 21.

8. Van Lommel, "Non-Local Consciousness," 15–16.

9. Bruce Greyson, "Varieties of Near-Death Experience," *Psychiatry* 56, no. 4 (November 1993): 390–399, https://pubmed.ncbi.nlm.nih.gov/8295976/; Daniel Kondziella, Jens P. Dreier, and Markus Harboe Olsen, "Prevalence of Near-Death Experiences in People with and without REM Sleep Intrusion," *PeerJ* 7 (August 27, 2019): e7585, https://peerj.com/articles/7585.

10. Dr. Ron Smothermon, phone interview with John Burke, May 13, 2022. Used with permission. Some quotes also taken from Dr. Ron Smothermon, "My Near-Death Experience during a Murder Attempt," (unpublished manuscript), Microsoft Word file. Used with permission.

11. "Arvind B NDE," Near-Death Experience Research Foundation (NDERF), accessed January 17, 2023, https://www.nderf.org/Experiences/1arvind_b_nde.html. NDERF excerpts used with permission of Jeffrey Long and Jody Long, founders and administrators of the Near-Death Experience Research Foundation.

12. Wendy Doniger, "Kali," *Encyclopedia Britannica*, last updated January 4, 2023, https://www.britannica.com/topic/Kali.

13. Cedric Kanana with Benjamin Fischer, *I Once Was Dead: How God Rescued Me from Islam, Drugs, Witchcraft, and Even Death* (Chicago: Oasis International, 2022), loc. 111–112, Kindle. Used with permission of Oasis International and Cedric Kanana. Swidiq later changed his name to Cedric when he converted to Christianity and became an Anglican priest.

14. Melanie McCullough, Zoom interview with John Burke, May 28, 2019. Used with permission.

15. Santosh Acharjee, phone interview with John Burke, November 15, 2022. Used with permission.

16. Heidi Barr, "Your Life Is in Good Hands," (unpublished manuscript), PDF. Used with permission.

17. Jim Woodford, phone interview with John Burke, December 9, 2022. Used with permission.

18. Susanne Seymoure, Zoom interview with John Burke, February 28, 2022. Used with permission.

19. "Sarah W Probable NDE," Near-Death Experience Research Foundation (NDERF), accessed January 17, 2023, https://www.nderf.org/Experiences/1sarah_w _probable_nde.html.

20. Erica McKenzie, *Dying to Fit In* (self-pub., CreateSpace, 2015), 85. Used with permission.

21. See Nancy Evans Bush, "Distressing Western Near-Death Experiences: Finding a Way through the Abyss," in *The Handbook of Near-Death Experiences*, 70.

22. Acharjee, phone interview with John Burke.

23. Woodford, phone interview with John Burke.

24. McKenzie, *Dying to Fit In*, 97.

25. C. S. Lewis, *The Quotable Lewis*, ed. Wayne Martindale and Jerry Root (Carol Stream, IL: Tyndale, 1989; 2012), 292.

26. When we read of God's "wrath" in the Bible, this is God's just punishment of prideful, stubborn rebellion against the Creator—to let the free will turned against God have its horrific consequences.

27. Dean Braxton, personal interview with John Burke, Austin, Texas, October 2, 2019. Used with permission.

28. Woodford, phone interview with John Burke.

29. Mark McDonough, "House Fire Kills Family and Burns Most of Surgeon's Body as Teen. Next, He Meets Them in Heaven," interview by Randy Kay, Randy Kay

Ministries, September 3, 2022, YouTube video, https://www.youtube.com/watch?v=DVdkjJA-Ycc&t=843s. Used with permission of Mark McDonough. Includes minor edits by Dr. Mark McDonough.

30. Mark D. McDonough, *Forged through Fire: A Reconstructive Surgeon's Story of Survival, Faith, and Healing* (Grand Rapids, MI: Revell, 2019), 75.

31. Cheri Henderson, "Dr. Mark McDonough: Burn Victim Turned Plastic Surgeon," *Orlando*, August 7, 2020, https://www.orlandomagazine.com/dr-mark-mcdonough-burn-victim-turned-plastic-surgeon/.

32. Dr. Mary Neal, personal interview with John Burke, Austin, Texas, February 22, 2016. Used with permission.

33. "Alexa H NDE," Near-Death Experience Research Foundation (NDERF), accessed January 20, 2023, https://www.nderf.org/Experiences/1alexa_h_nde.html. Used with permission. Includes minor edits and additions by Alexa Hartung sent to Kathy Burke via email, January 5, 2023.

34. Dean Braxton, personal interview with John Burke, Austin, Texas, September 26, 2019. Used with permission.

35. Crystal McVea and Alex Tresniowski, *Waking Up in Heaven: A True Story of Brokenness, Heaven, and Life Again* (New York: Howard Books, 2013), loc. 1, 89–91, Kindle.

36. McKenzie, *Dying to Fit In*, loc. 73–74, Kindle.

37. Heidi Barr, phone interview with John Burke, September 20, 2022. Used with permission.

38. Rebecca Ruter Springer, *Intra Muros* (Elgin, IL: David C. Cook Publishing, 1898), 91.

About the Author

JOHN BURKE is the author of the *New York Times* bestseller *Imagine Heaven*, along with *Imagine the God of Heaven*, *No Perfect People Allowed*, *Soul Revolution*, and *Unshockable Love*. He and his wife, Kathy, founded Gateway Church, a multisite church based in Austin, Texas, that helps people explore faith. As an international speaker, John has addressed hundreds of thousands of people in thirty countries on topics of leadership, spiritual growth, and the exhilarating life to come. John and Kathy have two children and two grandchildren.

JOIN JOHN BURKE AND DISCOVER THE GOD WHO LOVES YOU DEEPLY AND IS CLOSER THAN YOU COULD EVER IMAGINE.

What nearly seventy near-death experiences reveal about the God of heaven

Great for small group or individual study

DVD to accompany the study guide with teaching from John Burke

A concise guide to commonly asked questions about near-death experiences